Strawberries

Victoria Blakemore

vblakemore.author@gmail.com

Copyright info/picture credits

Cover, teressa/AdobeStock; Page 3, Storyblocks; Page 5, ulleo/Pixabay; Page 7, Vasia24/Pixabay; Page 9, WerbeFabrik/Pixabay; Page 11, Storyblocks; Page 13, Davies_Designs/Pixabay; Page 15, Couleur/Pixabay; Page 17, Storyblocks; Page 19, juergen64/Pixabay; Page 21, Storyblocks; Page 23; Carl-Stridsberg/Pixabay; Page 25, fpaulus/Pixabay; Page 27, Storyblocks; Page 29, Storyblocks; Page 31, teressa/AdobeStock; Page 33, Ajale/Pixabay

Table of Contents

What Are Strawberries?

Strawberries are fruits. They are members of the rose family. Some other members of the rose family are apples, pears, and plums.

They are thought of as a super fruit because of the high number of **nutrients** they have.

Strawberries are not actually berries. Their seeds are on the outside, not inside like true berries.

History of Strawberries

Strawberries are **native** to many parts of the world. The most common kind is originally from North America. It was brought to Europe in the 1600's.

Ancient Romans believed that strawberries could be used as medicine. They were used to treat fevers and infections.

4

Before the 1800's, most strawberries were wild. When they became more popular, people started to **cultivate** their own.

Strawberry Stems

It may look like strawberries grow on vines, but they don't. The strawberry plant has long stems that make it look like a vine.

The stems of strawberry plants are soft. They are not hard enough to make the plant stand up.

The stem transports **nutrients** from

the soil to the rest of the plant.

Strawberry Leaves

The strawberry plant leaves have an important job. They **absorb** sunlight and turn it into **energy** for the plant.

This process is called **photosynthesis** and the plant could not grow without it.

Strawberry plant leaves are very

large. This helps them to absorb

lots of sunlight.

Strawberry Flowers

Strawberry plants grow small flowers. Most are white with yellow centers.

The flowers are where the strawberries grow from on the plant. The strawberries will grow just under where the flowers were on the stem.

Flowers must be **pollinated** for the strawberries to grow. Bees are very important for plants, including the strawberry plant.

Strawberry Flesh

The strawberry flesh is the part that we eat. It is under the leafy cap, or **calyx**, where the strawberry is connected to the stem.

When it is **ripe**, it is usually bright red in color. It is also firm. Inside the strawberry is usually pale red and white in color.

A quick way to remove the **calyx** from the strawberry is using a straw. Stick the straw through the bottom of the strawberry and the top will pop off.

Strawberry Seeds

Strawberry seeds are different

from many other plant seeds.

The small bumps on the outside

of the strawberry are actually

tiny fruits, not the seeds!

The tiny fruits are called

"achenes." The strawberry

seeds are stored inside the

achenes.

Strawberries can have hundreds

of seeds. Most have about 200.

Life Cycle

Strawberry seeds are planted in soil. If they have enough water and nutrients, they will start to sprout.

When a plant starts to sprout, the roots grow down into the soil. The stem grows up out of the soil. The stem will grow leaves and flowers.

Strawberry buds will start to

grow on the end of the stems.

They take about three days to

go from white to red.

17

Strawberries are grown in many different parts of the world. They can be grown on every continent except Antarctica.

The United States grows more strawberries than any other country, followed by Spain.

Strawberries are grown in every state of the United States. California grows the most. One billion pounds of strawberries are grown there every year.

Growing Strawberries

Strawberries are usually planted between autumn and early spring. In places where it gets very cold, they need to be planted after winter.

They are ready to harvest in the spring. Many are ready to pick four to six weeks after the flowers bloom.

Strawberries are often grown in rows in large fields. The rows allow people to walk between them for harvesting.

Harvesting

Strawberries are very **delicate**. They need to be harvested by hand to keep them **intact**.

Strawberries that are ready to be picked are **ripe**. The ripe strawberries are picked by hand and put in baskets, buckets, or boxes.

The strawberries need to be refrigerated soon after they are picked. This helps to keep them fresh.

Transportation

Strawberries that have been picked and cooled are ready to be sold. They are quickly loaded into special refrigerated trucks.

The trucks keep the strawberries cold . They are brought to market quickly so they are fresh when they are sold.

Strawberries are sometimes shipped in large crates. Other times, they are packaged into smaller containers to be sold.

Markets

Strawberries are sold in grocery stores, fruit markets, and at roadside stands.

At some farms, people can pay to pick their own strawberries. The strawberries they pick are weighed and they pay a price per pound.

Most people get their strawberries from grocery stores or markets.

Nutrition

Strawberries are full of vitamins C, B, and A. They are also rich in **minerals** like manganese, potassium, and magnesium.

They also provide your body with fiber, calcium, and iron. Even though strawberries are sweet, they are very low in sugar.

Strawberries are a very healthy

snack. They are low in sugar, fat,

and **calories**.

Health Benefits

Strawberries provide your body with a lot of **nutrients**. They can help your heart to be healthy and lower blood pressure.

It is also thought that parts of strawberries can reduce the risk of getting some kinds of cancer.

Strawberries can also help to whiten your teeth. The acids in strawberries can remove stains.

Eating Strawberries

Strawberries can be used in many different foods. They are used in foods like smoothies, fruit salad, pies, cakes, jams, and ice cream.

They can also be added to other foods like pancakes or yogurt. Many people also eat strawberries with chocolate.

Glossary

Absorb: to take in

Calories: units of energy

Calyx: the top of the strawberry where it is attached to the stem

Cultivate: to plant and help grow

Delicate: easy to break or hurt

Energy: the power to make something work or be active

Intact: whole, undamaged

Minerals: substances that our bodies need to grow and work

Native: a place where something

came from

Nutrients: something in food that helps

people, animals, and plants grow

Photosynthesis: the process of a plant

turning sunlight into energy

Pollinated: when pollen is moved from

one plant to another, allowing crops

to grow

Produced: made, grown

Ripe: ready to be eaten

About the Author

Victoria Blakemore is a first grade

teacher in Southwest Florida with a

passion for reading.

You can visit her at

www.elementaryexplorers.com

Also in This Series

Gray Wolves	Sloths	Flamingos	Camels	Koalas	Honey Bees
Pandas	Pangolins	White-Tailed Deer	Orcas	Giraffes	Corn
Meerkats	Echidnas	Walruses	Raccoons	Bald Eagles	Apples
Arctic Foxes	Red Pandas	Cassowaries	Tigers	Ladybugs	Moose
Beluga Whales	Leopards	Elephants	Jellyfish	Binturongs	Lions
Dolphins	Reindeer	Hammerhead Sharks	Hippos	Pumpkins	Peafowl

Victoria Blakemore

Elementary Explorers

Also in This Series

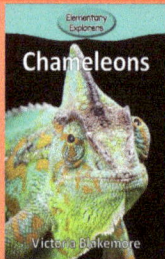

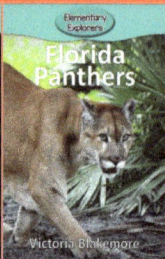

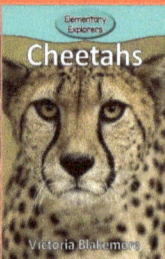

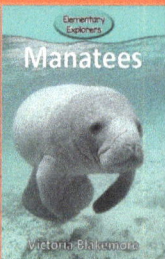

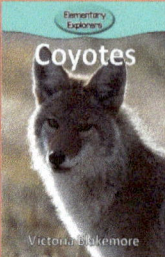

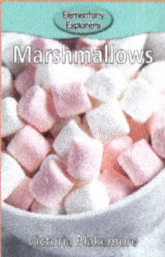

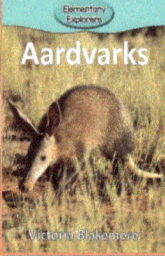

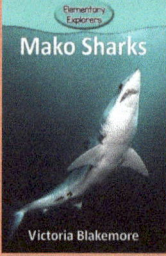

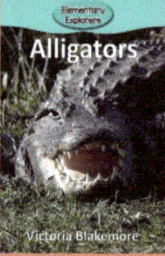

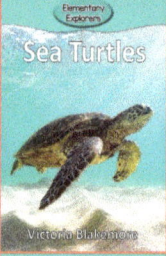

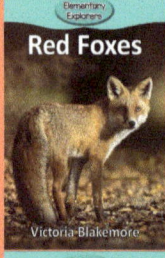

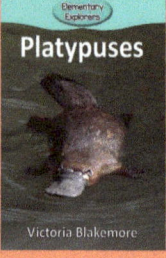

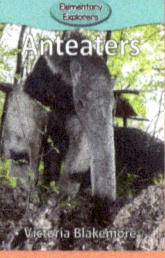

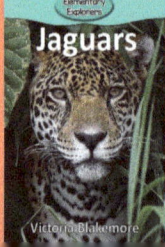

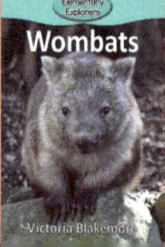

Chameleons	Florida Panthers	Aye-Ayes	Black Bears	Cheetahs	Manatees
Gingerbread	Polar Bears	Hot Chocolate	Orangutans	Coyotes	Marshmallows
Strawberries	Aardvarks	Mako Sharks	Alligators	Frogs	Hedgehogs
Brown Bears	Bongos	Sea Turtles	Quokkas	Muskrats	Zebras
Red Foxes	Ring-Tailed Lemurs	Platypuses	Anteaters	Kangaroos	Rhinos
Jaguars	Wombats				

www.ingramcontent.com/pod-product-compliance
Lightning Source LLC
Chambersburg PA
CBHW051254020426
42333CB00025B/3201